THANK YOU FOR BUYING MY BOOK!

COLOR • CUT • WRITE • GLUE
DOODLE • CREATE • SHARE

USE THIS BOOK TO CREATE YOUR OWN
PRETTY ART. WRITE A NOTE, SHARE AN IDEA
AND CREATE SOMETHING SPECIAL. PUT THE PIECES
TOGETHER HOWEVER YOU'D LIKE.
THERE ARE TEMPLATES TO HELP YOU, ART
TO INSPIRE YOU AND WORDS TO MOTIVATE YOU.

HAPPY CREATING!

jen

JEN GOODE
100DIRECTIONS.COM

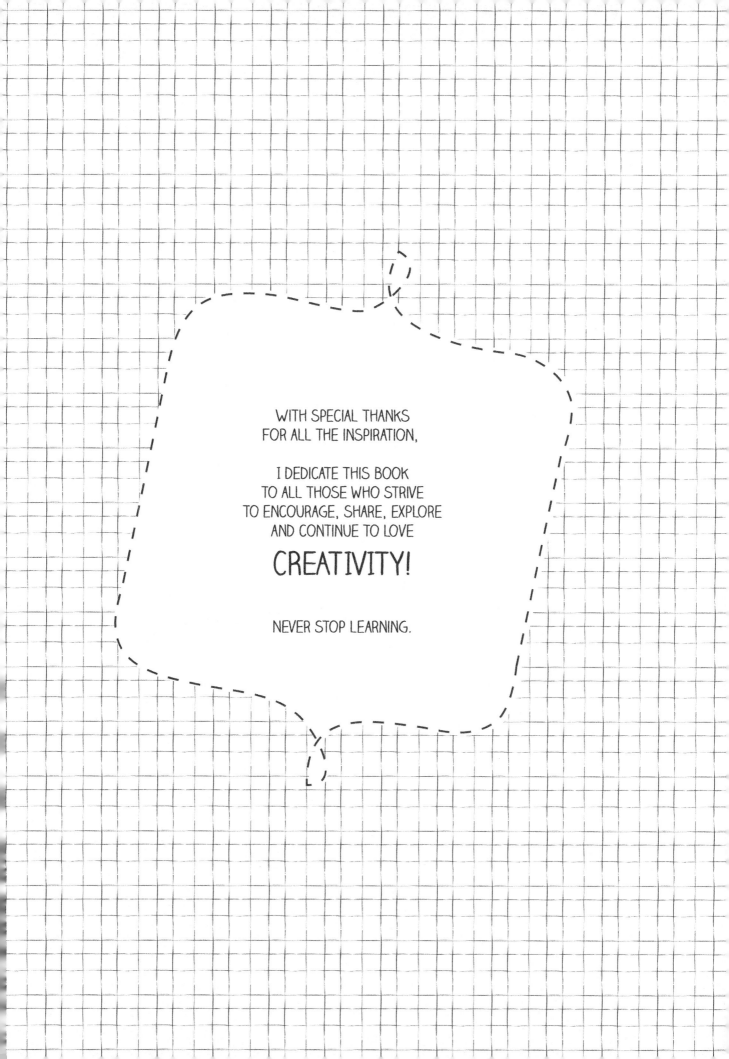

WITH SPECIAL THANKS
FOR ALL THE INSPIRATION,

I DEDICATE THIS BOOK
TO ALL THOSE WHO STRIVE
TO ENCOURAGE, SHARE, EXPLORE
AND CONTINUE TO LOVE

CREATIVITY!

NEVER STOP LEARNING.

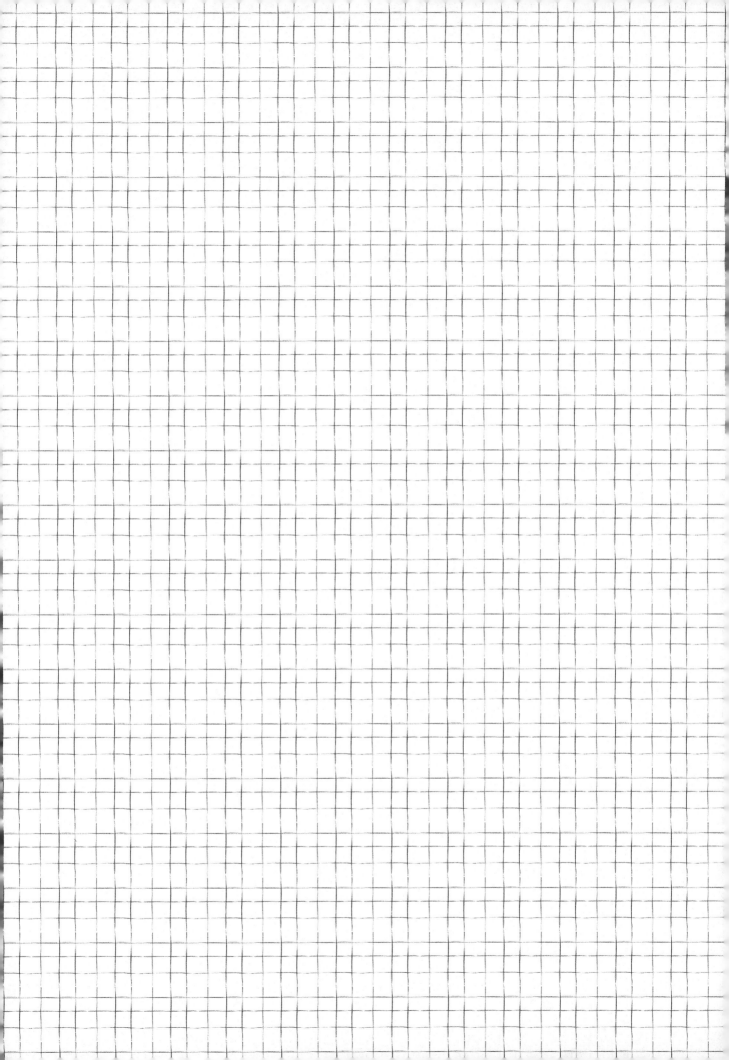

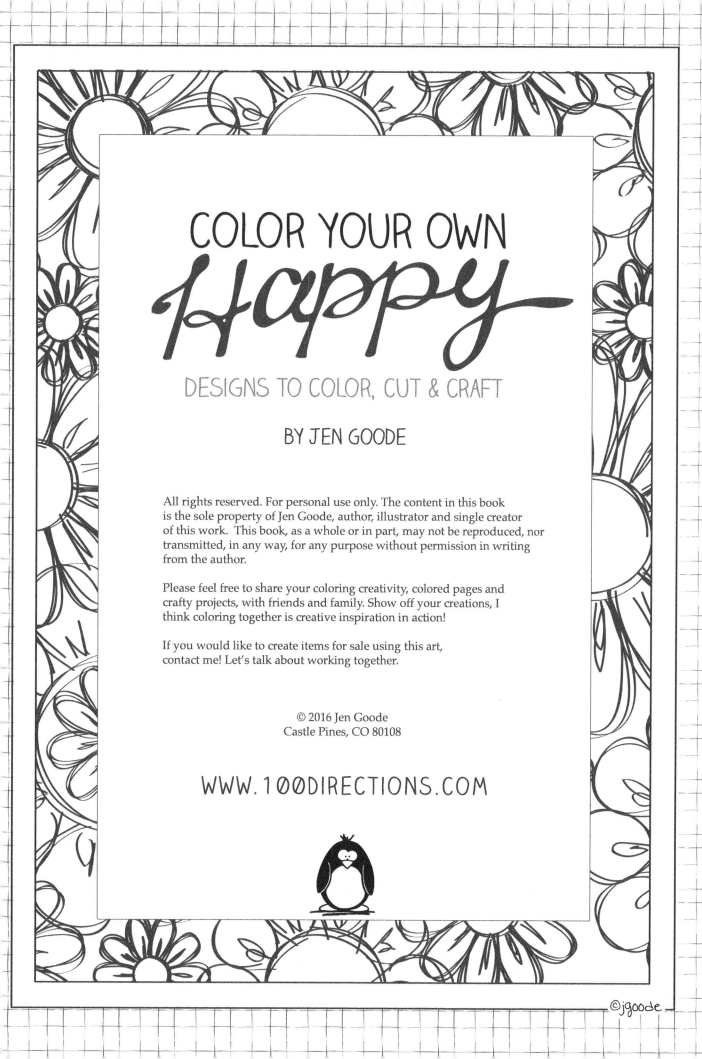

COLOR YOUR OWN
Happy

DESIGNS TO COLOR, CUT & CRAFT

BY JEN GOODE

© 2016 Jen Goode
Castle Pines, CO 80108

WWW.100DIRECTIONS.COM

©jgoode

©jgoode

©jgoode

©jgoode

©jgoode

©jgoode

©jgoode

©jgoode

©jgoode

©jgoode

©jgoode

©jgoode

©jgoode

©jgoode

©jgoode

©jgoode

Happiness is

©jgoode

©jgoode

©jgoode

©jgoode

@jgoode

©jgoode

©jgoode

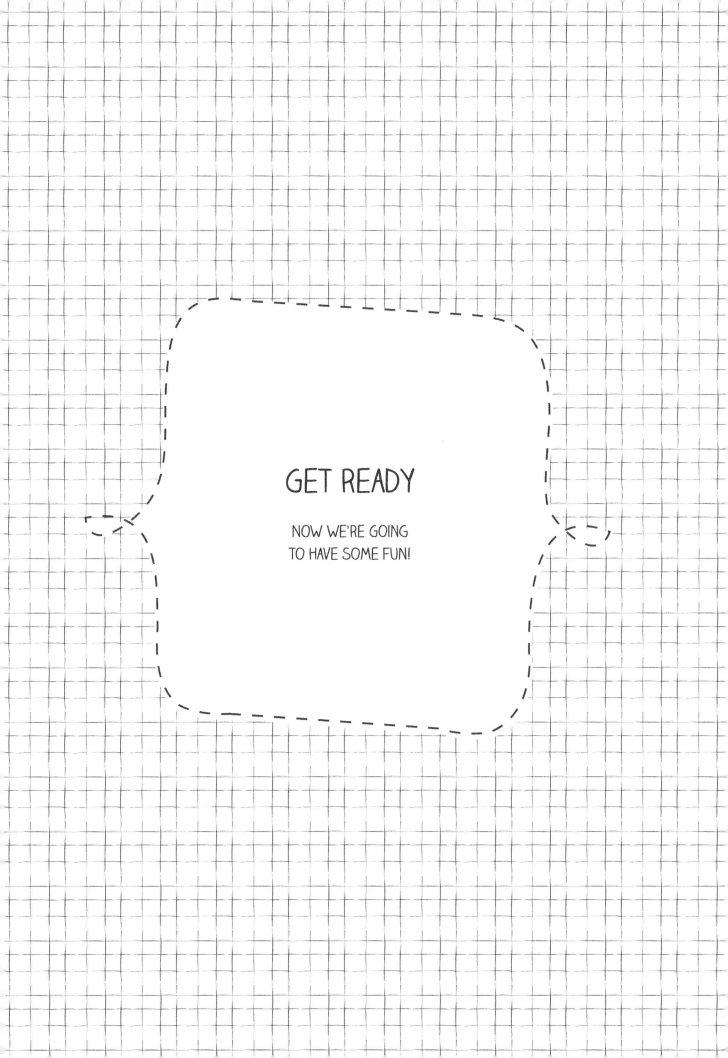

GET READY

NOW WE'RE GOING
TO HAVE SOME FUN!

MAKE STUFF WITH YOUR COLORED PAGES

I'VE INCLUDED SOME IDEAS OF THINGS YOU CAN MAKE WITH THE PAGES YOU COLOR IN THIS BOOK. THERE ARE INSTRUCTIONS AND TEMPLATES TO HELP YOU GET STARTED. YOU CAN ADD EXTRAS LIKE GLITTER OR HAND STITCHING TO MAKE YOUR CREATIONS EVEN MORE... YOU.

FOR MORE IDEAS AND TEMPLATES BEYOND THIS BOOK, VISIT MY BLOG

100DIRECTIONS.COM

TIP
COPY YOUR COLORED ART BEFORE YOU CUT OUT FOR CRAFTS SO YOU CAN USE THE SAME ART AGAIN

©jgoode

©jgoode

©jgoode

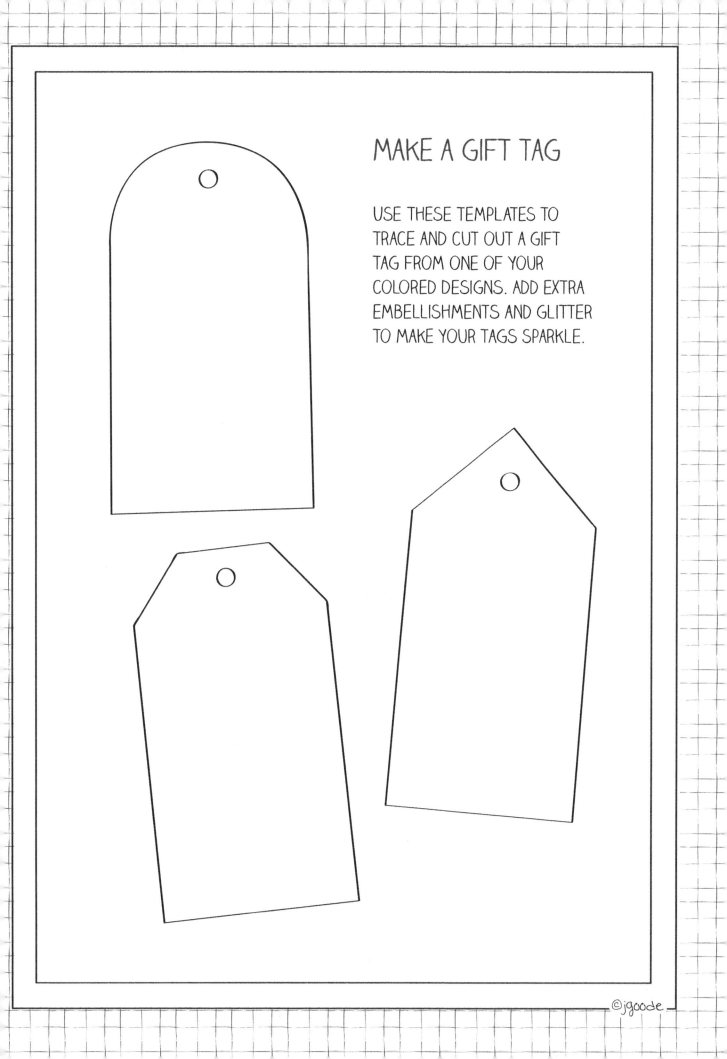

MAKE A GIFT TAG

USE THESE TEMPLATES TO
TRACE AND CUT OUT A GIFT
TAG FROM ONE OF YOUR
COLORED DESIGNS. ADD EXTRA
EMBELLISHMENTS AND GLITTER
TO MAKE YOUR TAGS SPARKLE.

©jgoode

DECORATE A T-SHIRT

METHOD 1

1. COPY YOUR COLORED DESIGN
   ON TO PRINTABLE T-SHIRT TRANSFER PAPER.

2. TRIM TRANSFER PAPER AS DESIRED.

3. FOLLOW TRANSFER PAPER INSTRUCTIONS
   TO TRANSFER DESIGN TO T-SHIRT FABRIC.

METHOD 2

1. COPY UN-COLORED DESIGN
   TO STANDARD PRINTER PAPER.

2. COLOR DESIGN WITH FABRIC CRAYONS.

3. FOLLOW CRAYON INSTRUCTIONS TO
   TRANSFER COLOR TO T-SHIRT FABRIC.

OPTIONAL

ADD FABRIC GLITTER OR RHINESTONES FOR EXTRA BLING.

©jgoode

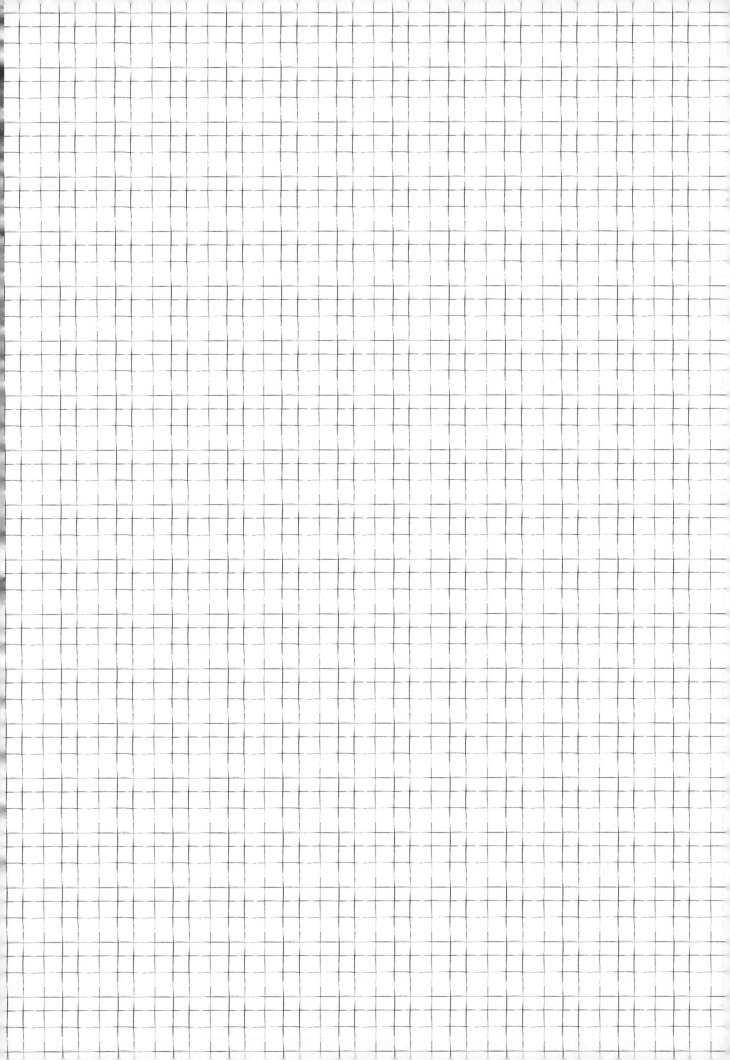

MAKE A BOOK MARK

I AM A BOOKMARK
TEMPLATE

1. CUT OUT AND
   TRIM TO THE SIZE
   YOU PREFER.

2. PUNCH A HOLE AT THE
   TOP OF THE BOOKMARK.

3. TIE A RIBBON
   THROUGH THE HOLE.

IF YOU WANT A THICKER
BOOKMARK, GLUE A FEW
LAYERS OF PAPER TOGETHER
OR GLUE COLORED ART TO
A PIECE OF CARDBOARD
AND THEN TRIM TO SIZE.

YOU CAN ALSO LAMINATE
THE BOOKMARK TO HELP
IT LAST A LITTLE LONGER.

©jgoode

BACK

STANDARD A2 NOTECARD
(5.5 X 4.25)

------ FOLD ------

YOU CAN USE THIS TEMPLATE TO CUT
OUT AND MAKE YOUR OWN CARD.

1. CUT OUT A COLORED PAGE.

2. TRIM TO FIT THIS CARD SIZE.

3. GLUE TO THE FRONT OF A CARD.

FRONT

©jgoode

MAKE A PRETTY PICTURE FRAME

4X6 PHOTO TEMPLATE

USE A COLORED PAGE TO DECORATE
A PICTURE. CUT OUT THIS CENTER
RECTANGLE "WINDOW" AND
PLACE THE PHOTO BEHIND THE OPENING.
TRIM OUTTER EDGE TO FIT YOUR FRAME.

4X6 WINDOW CUT LINE

4X6 PHOTO

©jgoode

MAKE A PRETTY PICTURE FRAME

5X7 PHOTO
TEMPLATE

USE A COLORED PAGE TO DECORATE A PICTURE.
CUT OUT THIS CENTER RECTANGLE "WINDOW"
AND PLACE THE PHOTO BEHIND THE OPENING.
TRIM OUTTER EDGE TO FIT YOUR FRAME.

5X7 WINDOW CUT LINE

5X7 PHOTO

©jgoode

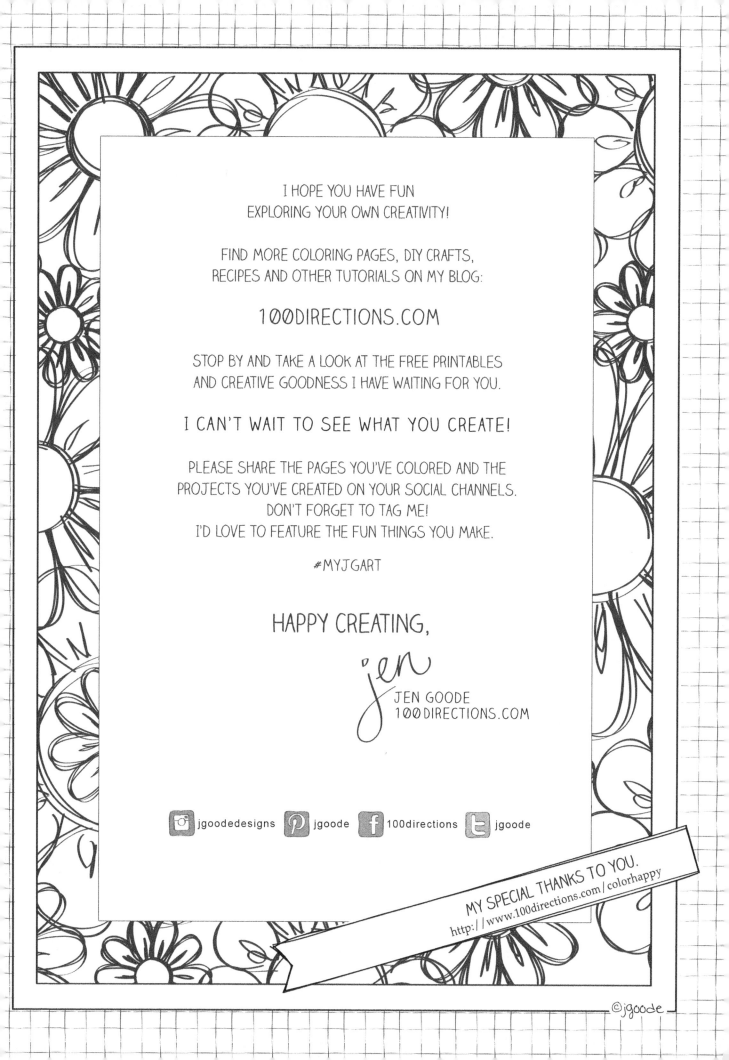

I HOPE YOU HAVE FUN
EXPLORING YOUR OWN CREATIVITY!

FIND MORE COLORING PAGES, DIY CRAFTS,
RECIPES AND OTHER TUTORIALS ON MY BLOG:

100DIRECTIONS.COM

STOP BY AND TAKE A LOOK AT THE FREE PRINTABLES
AND CREATIVE GOODNESS I HAVE WAITING FOR YOU.

I CAN'T WAIT TO SEE WHAT YOU CREATE!

PLEASE SHARE THE PAGES YOU'VE COLORED AND THE
PROJECTS YOU'VE CREATED ON YOUR SOCIAL CHANNELS.
DON'T FORGET TO TAG ME!
I'D LOVE TO FEATURE THE FUN THINGS YOU MAKE.

#MYJGART

HAPPY CREATING,

jen

JEN GOODE
100DIRECTIONS.COM

jgoodedesigns   jgoode   100directions   jgoode

MY SPECIAL THANKS TO YOU.
http://www.100directions.com/colorhappy

©jgoode

ABOUT THE ARTIST

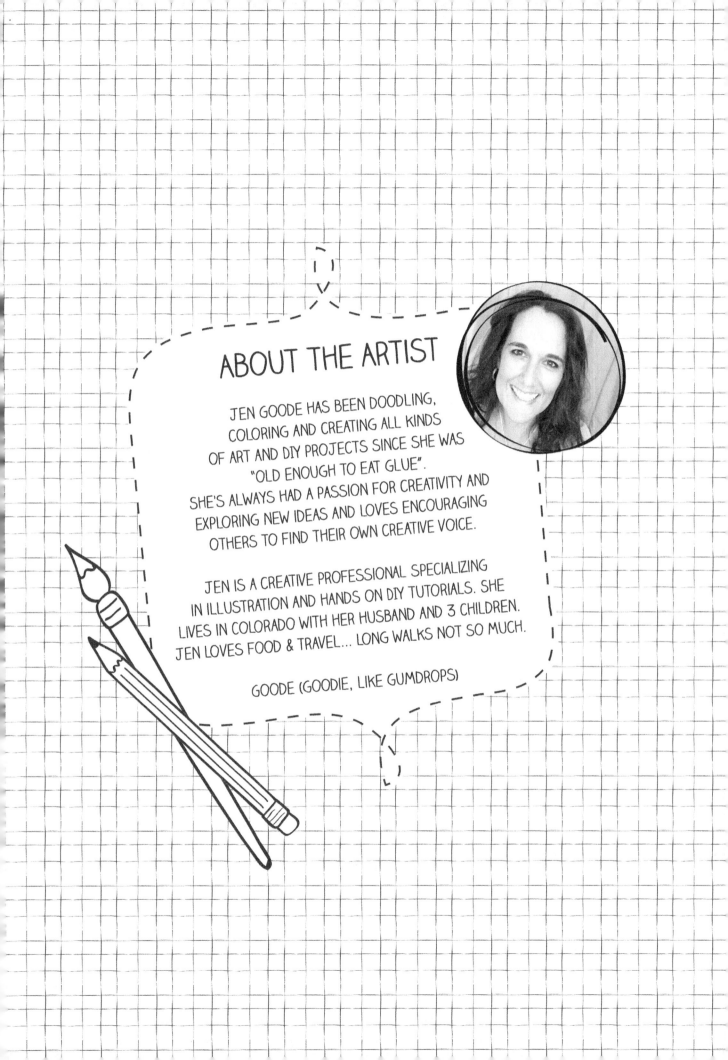

JEN GOODE HAS BEEN DOODLING,
COLORING AND CREATING ALL KINDS
OF ART AND DIY PROJECTS SINCE SHE WAS
"OLD ENOUGH TO EAT GLUE".
SHE'S ALWAYS HAD A PASSION FOR CREATIVITY AND
EXPLORING NEW IDEAS AND LOVES ENCOURAGING
OTHERS TO FIND THEIR OWN CREATIVE VOICE.

JEN IS A CREATIVE PROFESSIONAL SPECIALIZING
IN ILLUSTRATION AND HANDS ON DIY TUTORIALS. SHE
LIVES IN COLORADO WITH HER HUSBAND AND 3 CHILDREN.
JEN LOVES FOOD & TRAVEL... LONG WALKS NOT SO MUCH.

GOODE (GOODIE, LIKE GUMDROPS)

Made in the USA
Monee, IL
10 December 2024

72627889R00050